AN APOLOGY TO MY YOUNGER SELF

A JOURNEY OF RESILIENCE AND REDISCOVERY

EVA ITUMELENG MALINGA

Table of Contents

Introduction

his book is dedicated to my teenage daughter, Bonolo, whose unwavering love and support have been a constant source of inspiration and strength. May you always remember that you are capable of achieving anything you set your mind to, and may you never lose sight of the incredible potential that lies within you.

And to all the other teens who are struggling with confidence, know that you are not alone. You are worthy, you are loved, and you are capable of overcoming any obstacle that comes your way. May this book serve as a guiding light on your journey to self-discovery and empowerment.

Together, let us explore the depths of the human experience, embracing the beauty of resilience, and celebrating the triumph of the human spirit. For it is in the darkest of nights that the stars shine brightest, illuminating the path forward with their unwavering light.

Chapter 1: A Confident Beginning

Dear Younger Me,

I want to take you back to our early years, to a time when confidence was our constant companion. In primary school, we were outgoing, full of dreams, and unafraid to face the world. Our days were filled with laughter, curiosity, and an unshakeable belief in ourselves. We thrived on challenges and delighted in the pride we saw in our mother's eyes.

Our family believed in us wholeheartedly. Every accomplishment, no matter how small, was celebrated with genuine joy and encouragement. They saw a bright future in us, often expressing how proud they were of our achievements and our fearless approach to life. We were the shining star of our home, a source of pride and inspiration for everyone around us.

Our dreams were limitless, and nothing seemed out of reach. We imagined ourselves achieving great things, and every day was another step toward those aspirations. Whether it was excelling in school, participating in sports, or engaging in creative projects, we faced each challenge with enthusiasm and confidence. We felt invincible, buoyed by the unwavering support and belief of our loved ones.

These early years were a golden period, where the world seemed full of possibilities and we felt empowered to chase our dreams. The love and encouragement from our family formed the foundation of our self-esteem, making us feel capable of conquering anything we set our minds to.

Chapter: 2 The Truth about my father

Then I remember when it all started, it started with the revelation of our dad. In primary school when I first discovered that the man I had always known as my father was, in fact, my stepfather. But unlike a quiet realization or a gentle conversation, the truth was revealed to me in the most dramatic and bewildering way.

It was a normal day, or so I thought. I was at home, doing what any child my age would be doing, without a care in the world. The phone rang, and my mother's friend, who happened to be visiting at the time, answered it. After a few moments of hushed conversation, she turned to me with an odd expression of excitement and confusion on her face.

With a wide smile, she said, "Your father is on the phone. He wants to talk to you!"

I froze. My father? My mind raced in confusion, trying to understand what she meant. How could my father be calling me when he was already at work, like every other day? The thought bounced around my head as I slowly took the phone from her.

"Hello?" I said cautiously, still puzzled by what was happening.

On the other end of the line, I heard a man's voice—a voice that sounded foreign, yet strangely familiar in a way I couldn't explain. His words were cheerful, excited even. "Hi! It's your father! I've been wanting to talk to you for so long."

My heart stopped. I pulled the phone away from my ear, staring at it as if it had just betrayed me. That voice didn't belong to the man I had called "Dad" my whole life. It was someone else entirely. I couldn't comprehend what was happening. There was no way this could be real, I thought. But the man's voice persisted, and with a growing sense of dread, I asked the only question that made sense in that moment.

"Who are you?"

He didn't hesitate. "I'm your biological father. I've been wanting to meet you."

The room suddenly felt too small, the air too thick. I didn't know what to say or how to process the flood of emotions that crashed over me like a tidal wave. The words "biological father" hit me with a force I wasn't prepared for. In that moment, my whole world shifted.

I looked over at my mother's friend, hoping she could make sense of what I had just heard, but she just smiled at me with a kind of nervous excitement, clearly thinking this was some sort of joyous reunion. But to me, it was anything but joyous. It felt like my reality had been torn open, exposing a truth I wasn't ready for.

Moments later, as if to cement this new reality, my mother came into the room. She took one look at my face, and I saw the flicker of recognition in her eyes—the same heaviness I had felt in my chest now mirrored in hers. That was the moment I knew it was true. The man on the phone, this stranger, was my real father.

Not long after that phone call, arrangements were made for me to meet him. I was nervous, terrified even. What would he look like? What would he say? What would I say? I wasn't sure I was ready to meet this man who had been absent from my life, this person who suddenly wanted to claim a role in it.

When I finally met him in person, the shock was no less overwhelming. There he stood, a man I had never seen before, yet here he was claiming to be my father. I remember scanning his face, looking for something—anything—that resembled me, that could connect us. But I felt nothing. No spark of recognition, no sense of belonging. Just emptiness. He smiled at me with an eagerness that made me uncomfortable, as though he expected me to feel joy, but all I could feel was confusion and a sense of betrayal.

This man, this stranger, wasn't the father I knew. The man I called Dad—the man who had been there for every scraped knee, every school project, every bedtime story—wasn't this person. He was the one at home, at work, doing the things dads do. And now, in this instant, I was being told that everything I had believed about my family wasn't entirely true. It felt like the ground beneath me had shifted, and I was left grasping for something solid to hold onto.

Looking back, I wish I could apologize to my younger self for how devastating that moment must have been. I wish I could wrap my arms around her and tell her that the confusion, the fear, the overwhelming sense of betrayal she felt, was valid. I wish I could explain to her that it was okay to be angry, to be hurt. That it wasn't fair for her to have her reality shattered like that, with no warning and no preparation.

I'm sorry for the way you had to find out, for the shock that rippled through your young heart and left you questioning everything you thought you knew. I'm sorry that the adults around you didn't realize how deeply this revelation would affect you, and how long it would take for you to make peace with it.

But I also want to offer you reassurance, my younger self. You would come to understand that family is not defined by biology alone. The father who raised you, who was there every day, was every bit your dad, no matter what bloodline said otherwise. And while the man who claimed to be your biological father had his own story and reasons for his absence, that wouldn't change the fact that you were already deeply loved by the father who had chosen to be in your life.

In time, you would learn that the complexity of these relationships didn't diminish the love you had from the family you grew up with. You would realize that you didn't have to choose between one truth and another—that both could exist in their own right. And most importantly, you would find peace with the understanding that the man who had raised you was your father in every way that truly mattered.

So, to my younger self, I say this: You were stronger than you realized in that moment. You faced a truth that could have broken you, but you didn't let it. And though it hurt, you would grow from it. You would come to see that love isn't always simple, but it is powerful. The father who raised you, and the man who shared your bloodline, both had their own places in your story. But in the end, it was the love and care you received that truly shaped the person you would become.

Chapter 3: The Turning Point

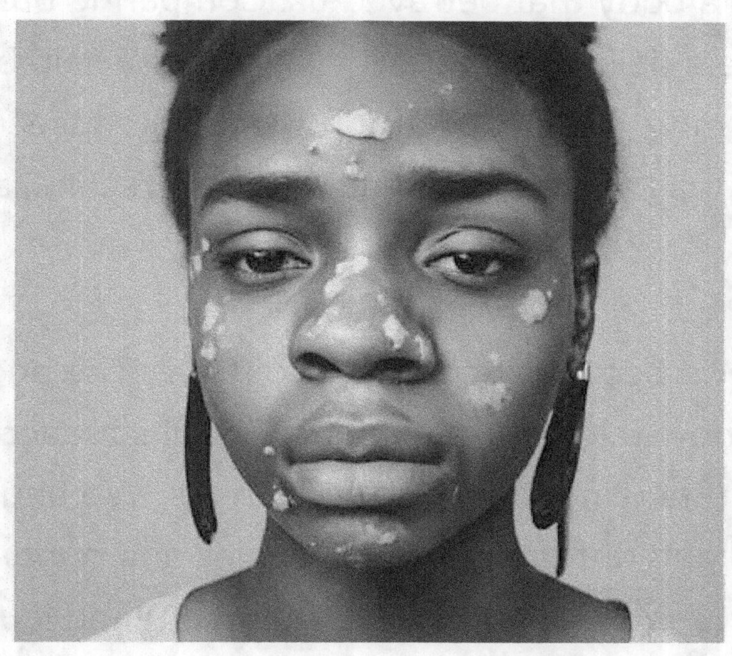

But then came the teenage years, a period that brought unexpected changes. We started developing acne, and with each new blemish, our confidence began to erode. The mirror became a source of dread rather than reflection. The outgoing, self-assured child faded, replaced by someone unsure and increasingly withdrawn.

Our body started to change in other ways too. We began developing breasts and experiencing the awkwardness of puberty. While our peers seemed to blossom into beautiful, confident young women, we felt trapped in a body that betrayed us. Comparing ourselves to others became a daily struggle, and we couldn't help but feel that we fell short. The more we looked around, the more it seemed that everyone else was effortlessly beautiful and graceful, amplifying our insecurities.

Facing the world became increasingly difficult. The once vibrant and fearless child now felt the urge to hide. Social situations that used to be enjoyable turned into daunting challenges. We began to shy away from the spotlight, retreating from activities and opportunities that once brought us joy. Our voice, once confident and loud, grew quieter as we struggled with our self-image.

But it wasn't just our social life that began to suffer. Our schoolwork, which once came naturally to us, started to slip. The focus and energy we once had for our studies seemed to fade. We found it increasingly hard to concentrate, often losing ourselves in thoughts of how we appeared to others. As our self-doubt grew, it affected everything, from homework to participation in class. We started skipping assignments, not because we didn't care, but because the weight of everything else felt too much to bear. Even though we eventually passed our exams, it wasn't with the excellence we once strived for. We knew deep down that we had the potential for more, but the burden of our insecurities held us back.

Facing people, especially new people, became a constant source of anxiety. Meeting new classmates, interacting with teachers, or even making small talk became tasks we dreaded. Every new face felt like a potential critic, someone who could see through the fragile mask of confidence we tried to wear. The fear of judgment became so overpowering that participating in class, something that once came so easily, turned into a struggle. The simple act of raising our hand felt like exposing ourselves to the world, vulnerable and uncertain.

There were times when we would sit in class, wanting to contribute but too afraid to speak. The words would get stuck in our throat, our mind racing with fears of sounding stupid or being ridiculed. And so, we remained silent, even when we knew the answers, letting the fear control us. This self-imposed isolation only deepened our insecurities, reinforcing the belief that we were not good enough to stand alongside our peers.

We started hiding ourselves, not just physically but emotionally as well. Layers of self-doubt and fear began to cover the bright spirit that used to shine so effortlessly. It was easier to withdraw than to face the potential judgment and rejection of others. The world, which once seemed so inviting, now felt like a place filled with obstacles and harsh reflections of our insecurities.

This period marked a significant turning point in our life. The confident, outgoing child who was the pride of our family began to disappear behind a veil of shyness and self-doubt. The once-clear path of academic success became clouded with uncertainty. It was a difficult and painful transition, one that made us question our worth and our place in the world.

Even though we made it through those years and passed, it was far from the shining success we had envisioned for ourselves. The external pressure combined with our internal battles left scars on our academic journey, and the struggle to face the world, particularly in social and academic settings, lingered long after. It was a harsh lesson in how quickly things could change, and how deeply self-doubt could affect every aspect of our life.

Chapter 4: Losing Opportunities

Our shyness grew, and with it came the loss of opportunities. We hesitated to speak up in class, avoided social gatherings, and missed out on forming deeper friendships. Our dreams, once so vibrant and within reach, seemed to slip further away. We began to feel disconnected from the person we once were, and it was heartbreaking to see how much we had changed.

As our self-esteem plummeted, so did our academic performance. Our grades, once a source of pride and validation, began to fall. The concentration and enthusiasm we once had for learning were overshadowed by our insecurities and the constant battle with our self-worth. Each poor mark felt like another confirmation of our inadequacies, deepening the spiral of self-doubt.

Despite all of this, our mother couldn't see the depth of our pain. It wasn't her fault—we had learned how to hide it so well. We masked our sadness behind smiles and pleasantries, ensuring that no one, not even the person closest to us, could see the cracks forming. While the rest of the family gathered together in the living room, laughing, watching TV, or sharing a meal, we preferred to retreat to our room. We found solace in isolation, where we didn't have to pretend to be okay.

Our room became our sanctuary. It was the only place where we didn't feel the pressure of pretending, where we could truly be alone with our thoughts. The silence and solitude gave us a strange sense of peace, even if it also deepened our loneliness. The idea of being surrounded by others, of having to engage in conversation or share in their happiness, became unbearable. More and more, we found ourselves drawn to the quiet, shutting the door and shutting the world out.

Sleep became our escape. During the day, it was easier to hide our pain, but at night, it felt inescapable. So, we would sleep. A lot. Sleep gave us peace, a break from the thoughts that plagued us during our waking hours. In those moments, we didn't have to feel the weight of our sadness, our insecurities, or the fear of never being enough. We would drift into slumber, hoping that maybe, just maybe, when we woke up, things would be better. But each day brought the same battles.

Unbeknownst to us, we were experiencing depression. The sadness and hopelessness that enveloped us were symptoms we didn't understand at the time. We thought it was just a phase, something we could push through, but it was far more than that. It was a heavy, suffocating blanket that we couldn't shake off. No amount of sleep or solitude could erase the feelings that continued to gnaw at us from the inside.

Nights were particularly hard. We often fell asleep crying, overwhelmed by a sense of despair and longing for the confidence and happiness we once had. Each month seemed to bring a new wave of tears and sleepless nights, where we wished for an escape from the relentless pressure of our insecurities. There were moments when we wished the world could just swallow us, to end the pain of feeling so out of place and undeserving.

Yet, no matter how much we withdrew, life continued. The opportunities we missed began to pile up—activities, friendships, even small moments of joy that passed us by while we were hidden away. The dreams we once had felt more distant with each passing day. The vibrant, ambitious version of ourselves seemed like a memory of a different person.

This chapter of our life was marked by the slow disappearance of opportunities—opportunities to grow, to connect, and to excel. Instead, we found ourselves trapped in a cycle of self-doubt, withdrawal, and quiet desperation. It was a battle we fought in silence, unseen by those around us, and even if we didn't fully understand it at the time, we were fighting a much larger war within ourselves.

Chapter 5: An Unbearable Loss

I know you're feeling overwhelmed right now, with the weight of the world pressing down on your shoulders. Navigating high school and dealing with the challenges of self-confidence is already tough, but life has dealt you not one, but two unimaginable blows.

Before your mother's passing, you faced another heartbreak—the loss of your grandmother. She wasn't just any grandmother; she was the person who fed your soul with happiness, the person who believed in you when everyone around you didn't. She was the one you would run to when you felt like the world was collapsing beside you. Her unwavering belief in you was like a shield against the doubts of others. She had a way of making you feel seen, understood, and unconditionally loved, even when it felt like the rest of the world was against you.

Losing her was devastating. Her absence left a hole in your heart, a silence where her reassuring words and gentle laughter used to be. You had lost the one person who made you feel like you could take on anything. And just as you were trying to cope with that heartache, life cruelly took another turn.

Your mother, your pillar of strength, passed away during your final year of school. The loss of these two incredible women in such a short time feels like the ground has been ripped from beneath you. The grief is overwhelming, compounded by the pressures of your final school year and the already heavy burden of self-doubt. You feel abandoned and alone, struggling to find the strength to continue without them by your side. The world seems colder, more intimidating without their comforting presence.

.

Your mother was more than just a parent. Like your grandmother, she believed in you when you couldn't believe in yourself. She had a way of lifting you up, of showing you your worth when your confidence faltered. Her passing leaves a void so deep that it feels like you're drowning in the emptiness. Nights are spent crying yourself to sleep, wondering how you'll ever move forward, how you'll ever face a future without the two women who shaped you, who held you together.

I know how your academic performance has been affected. Your grades, already impacted by your battles with confidence, have plummeted further as you find it increasingly difficult to concentrate and summon the motivation to study. You are carrying the weight of two losses now, two souls you loved more than anything.

But even in the darkest moments, there are glimpses of their love. In the quiet, you can hear their voices, your grandmother's soothing reassurance and your mother's gentle encouragement. They are with you still, pushing you to keep going, to find strength even when it seems impossible. These fleeting moments of connection become a lifeline, a reminder that they are still part of you, living on in your heart and memories.

Navigating this period of intense grief and loss will become a pivotal chapter in your journey. It will force you to confront your deepest fears and vulnerabilities, to seek out new sources of strength within yourself, and to begin the long and arduous process of healing. Though you feel lost without them, you will slowly start to find your way, driven by the desire to honor their memories and make them proud.

.

This chapter of your life is marked by profound sorrow, but it also becomes a turning point. It sets the stage for the subsequent chapters, where you will begin to rebuild your life, find new sources of support and love, and ultimately discover the resilience and inner strength that have been within you all along.

Hold on to the memories of your mother and your grandmother. Let them be a source of strength for you. Their spirits live on in you, and they would want you to continue fighting, to continue growing, and to continue pursuing your dreams. This is not the end of your story, but rather the beginning of a new chapter—one where you emerge stronger, more resilient, and ready to face whatever life throws your way.

Chapter 6: Finding Myself Again

Yet, through these struggles, we learned valuable lessons. We discovered that self-worth isn't tied to our appearance or the approval of others. We began to understand that true confidence comes from within, from accepting ourselves as we are and embracing our unique journey.

Our healing journey took a significant turn when we met the man of our dreams. He saw the beauty and potential in us that we had long forgotten. Even when we couldn't love ourselves, he loved us with a depth and sincerity that began to heal our wounded spirit. His unwavering support and affection became a lifeline, rescuing our soul from the depths of despair.

From the very beginning, his emotional connection with us was something that felt almost magical. He had a way of understanding us, of knowing what we needed even when we couldn't find the words to express it ourselves. His ability to connect with our heart was like nothing we had ever experienced before. When we were with him, we didn't have to hide. We didn't have to pretend to be anything other than who we were. He made us feel seen, and more importantly, he made us feel loved.

But as much as his love uplifted us, there were moments when it also scared us. The depth of his affection was something we had never felt before, and it was overwhelming at times. We had spent so many years convincing ourselves that we were unworthy of such devotion that accepting it felt terrifying. There was a fear of losing this love, of somehow not being good enough to keep it. Yet, he was patient, understanding our fears and insecurities, and never once did he make us feel guilty for them.

He was so gentle with our heart. He knew the pain we had carried for so long, the wounds that hadn't yet fully healed, and he handled us with care. There was never a moment when we felt pressured or pushed beyond what we were ready for. Instead, he gave us the time and space we needed to grow into this new version of ourselves, the one that was capable of accepting love and giving it in return. In his presence, we felt safe, not just physically but emotionally. For the first time in a long while, we felt like we could trust someone with our heart, with all the broken pieces we had tried so hard to hide.

He made us see life in a new light. What once seemed dark and hopeless was now filled with possibilities. His love was like sunshine breaking through the clouds, illuminating parts of us that had been hidden for so long. With him by our side, life didn't seem as overwhelming anymore. We began to dream again, to hope for things we had given up on, and to see the future as something bright and full of promise.

What stood out most about him was his unwavering commitment. He wasn't just saying the words to make us feel better; he was willing to build a life with us. Every day, through his actions, he showed us that he was in it for the long haul. He wanted a future with us, and he made that clear from the start. His promises were not empty; they were filled with intent and love. He told us one day he would make us his wife, and the mother of his children, and he never wavered from that promise.

Even when we doubted ourselves, he remained steadfast, always reminding us that we were worth fighting for. His consistency was a balm to our fragile self-esteem, and it slowly helped us believe in the possibility of a future filled with love and happiness. He wasn't just a partner; he was a builder, patiently helping us rebuild the parts of ourselves that had been shattered by years of self-doubt and fear.

He kept his promise. In time, we stood at the altar, becoming his wife, and later, the mother of his children. And through it all, he never stopped being that same man who connected with us so deeply, who loved us with tenderness and care. His love didn't just rescue us; it allowed us to rediscover who we truly were. He was the mirror reflecting the best parts of ourselves, parts that we had long forgotten existed.

With him, we found the courage to step out of the shadows and embrace life again. His belief in us gave us the strength to pursue our dreams, to take risks we wouldn't have taken before, and to face the world with newfound confidence. The love and stability he provided became the foundation upon which we built a new life—one filled with joy, purpose, and endless possibilities.

Through this relationship, we learned to be kind to ourselves, to focus on our strengths, and to pursue our dreams with renewed determination. His love not only rescued our soul but also reignited the spark within us, allowing us to rediscover the fearless dreamer we once were. We finally found ourselves again, and we did so in the arms of a man who made us feel like we were always enough

.

With time, we realized that we could overcome the insecurities and doubts that had held us back for so long. We found a new path, one marked by resilience, self-acceptance, and the unshakable support of the man who loved us back to life.

Chapter 7: Overcoming Challenges as a Parent

As we embarked on the journey of parenthood, our lives were forever changed by the arrival of our daughter, Bonolo, our beautiful princess. From the moment she came into the world, she captivated everyone who met her with her radiant beauty. Her soft, glowing skin and bright eyes filled with wonder made her stand out. People would often comment on how strikingly beautiful she was, and we couldn't have been more proud to be her parents.

However, with Bonolo's beauty came an unexpected challenge—doubt. People would often look at us and wonder aloud if we were ready, if we were capable of taking care of such a perfect little soul. Questions of our ability to raise her were whispered behind our backs, with others voicing their skepticism about whether we could handle the responsibility of motherhood. They doubted if we had the maturity, the patience, or the wisdom needed to nurture someone so delicate and full of promise.

At first, these doubts weighed heavily on us. The whispers of doubt made us question ourselves, even if just for a moment. Were we truly ready to be parents to such an extraordinary child? Could we offer Bonolo everything she needed and deserved? But deep down, we knew that we had more than enough love, commitment, and strength to raise her with all the care in the world.

As time passed, our actions silenced those doubts. We poured our heart and soul into being the best mother we could be to Bonolo, and soon, everyone who had once questioned us began to see the truth. They watched with surprise and admiration as we cared for her with such tenderness, patience, and understanding. Each day with Bonolo was filled with joy, love, and learning, and the bond between us only grew stronger. It became clear that we were not only capable of being her mother, but we excelled in it.

Motherhood brought out a new strength in us, a strength we hadn't even known we possessed. Despite the challenges we faced, we rose to meet them head-on because Bonolo's presence gave us a sense of purpose and belonging that we had never felt before. Her giggles, her small hand wrapped around our finger, and the way she looked up at us with trust and love—it was everything we needed to feel whole again.

Bonolo didn't just bring joy into our lives; she gave us a sense of belonging. For so long, we had struggled with feelings of inadequacy, uncertainty, and a loss of identity. But with her, we found our place in the world. Being her mother gave us a role that felt right, that fit us in ways nothing else ever had. It was in those quiet moments with her, when we would sit together in the stillness of the night or laugh at her playful antics, that we realized how truly blessed we were. She was our heart, and caring for her became the most fulfilling part of our life.

She helped us to see the beauty in life once again. The simple moments—her first steps, her first words—became monumental milestones, each one filling us with pride and wonder. With Bonolo, we felt like we had a reason to keep pushing forward, to fight through the hardships, and to build a life filled with love, not just for ourselves, but for her.

Yet, life had more challenges in store for us. As we embraced motherhood with open arms, we also faced the heartbreak of two miscarriages. After Bonolo, we wanted to expand our family and give her a sibling, but fate had other plans. Losing two pregnancies was a painful reminder of how fragile life can be, and it tested us in ways we weren't prepared for. The grief of those losses was profound, and we found ourselves questioning everything—our bodies, our faith, and our future as parents.

Despite the pain, Bonolo remained our constant source of light. In the moments when it felt like the grief would consume us, we would look at her, and her presence reminded us of all we had to be thankful for. She was the proof that we were strong, that we were capable of overcoming loss, and that life, even with its hardships, was still filled with beauty. She helped us find peace in the midst of our sorrow, and for that, we were forever grateful.

Through the ups and downs, we discovered that being Bonolo's mother was not just a role—it was our calling. And as we watched her grow, so did our own strength and confidence as a parent. The people who had once doubted us were now the ones expressing their amazement at the love and care we provided. They saw how we had not only met the challenges of motherhood but thrived in them, raising a beautiful, joyful, and kind child who was a reflection of the love that surrounded her.

Our journey as parents has been anything but easy, yet it has been the most rewarding path we've ever walked. Bonolo's existence gave us a renewed sense of belonging, a place in the world where we were truly needed, wanted, and loved. Her beauty wasn't just on the outside; it was in the way she filled our home with laughter, in the way she brought people together, and in how she gave us the strength to keep going, no matter what life threw our way.

As we look back now, we see that being Bonolo's mother was one of the greatest gifts we could ever receive. And though the journey has been marked by both joy and sorrow, it has also been filled with love, resilience, and an unbreakable bond between mother and daughter.

Chapter 8: Embracing New Opportunities

With the newfound confidence and support from our partner, we embarked on an exciting new chapter by pursuing higher education. College became not just a place of academic learning, but also a journey of self-discovery and personal growth. Surrounded by like-minded individuals and fueled by a thirst for knowledge, we thrived in this vibrant environment.

In college, we had the opportunity to meet new friends who embraced us for who we were. Through shared experiences and deep conversations, we formed bonds that would last a lifetime. These friendships provided invaluable support and encouragement, further bolstering our confidence and sense of belonging.

As we delved into our studies, we saw the world through a new lens—one filled with possibility and optimism. The challenges we encountered were no longer barriers but rather opportunities for growth and exploration. We embraced each new experience with enthusiasm, eager to uncover the endless opportunities that lay before us.

Amidst the excitement of college life, we also experienced a profound spiritual awakening. Through introspection and reflection, we found solace and purpose in our faith. Accepting Jesus as our savior brought a newfound sense of peace and clarity to our lives. His teachings of love, forgiveness, and compassion became guiding principles that shaped our interactions with others and our outlook on the world.

College became a transformative journey—a time of intellectual, emotional, and spiritual growth. It was here that we not only discovered our academic passions but also deepened our understanding of ourselves and our place in the world. With each new day, we embraced the opportunities that college offered, grateful for the chance to expand our horizons and become the person we were always meant to be.

Chapter 9: Nurturing Self-Love and Acceptance

Amidst the busyness of life, we made a conscious effort to prioritize self-care and self-love. After the hardships we had endured, we realized the importance of nurturing our own well-being. It became clear that in order to fully show up for our loved ones, we first needed to love and accept ourselves.

Slowly but surely, we began to rebuild our relationship with ourselves. We made an effort to look at our reflection in the mirror each day, to truly see the person staring back. Initially, it was a challenge to face the mirror, as it brought back memories of the insecurities and self-doubt that had plagued our teenage years. But with time, these moments of self-reflection became acts of self-compassion and acceptance.

r

As we looked deeper into the mirror, we began to see ourselves in a new light. We questioned why we had ever doubted our worth, why we had allowed our insecurities to overshadow our true beauty. Each day, the reflection looking back at us seemed to radiate more confidence and grace. We saw a very beautiful woman, not just in appearance, but in strength, resilience, and spirit.

This journey of self-discovery was deeply empowering. We realized that our worth was not determined by external validations or comparisons with others. Instead, it was rooted in our unique experiences, strengths, and the love we carried within us. By embracing our true selves, we found a sense of inner peace and contentment that we had long sought.

Through practices like mindfulness, gratitude, and self-reflection, we cultivated a deep sense of inner peace and acceptance. We learned to celebrate our accomplishments, no matter how small, and to be gentle with ourselves during moments of struggle. By nurturing our relationship with ourselves, we found that we were better able to show up fully for our loved ones and for the world around us.

This period marked a significant turning point in our journey. We no longer sought validation from others, but instead, found it within ourselves. By loving and accepting ourselves, we unlocked a new level of confidence and happiness. And as we embraced this newfound self-love, we radiate positivity and strength, inspiring those around us to do the same.

Chapter 10: Paying It Forward

Inspired by our own transformation, we felt compelled to pay it forward and support others on their journey to self-discovery and confidence. Whether through mentorship, volunteering, or simply offering a listening ear, we found fulfillment in empowering others to overcome their own challenges and embrace their true potential.

Reflecting on our own experiences, we began to reach out to teenagers who were grappling with the same insecurities and self-doubt that had once consumed us. We wanted to share the lessons we had learned and offer guidance and encouragement to help them navigate their own journeys. We knew firsthand how difficult it could be to face the world when you felt inadequate, and we were determined to make a difference.

Our message to these young individuals was clear: never let your appearance define your worth. We encouraged them to look beyond the surface and to recognize the unique qualities that made them special. Each of us is beautifully unique in our own way, and it is our individuality that makes us who we are. What truly matters is what lies within our hearts and how we choose to view the world around us.

We shared our story of overcoming adversity, emphasizing that true beauty and worth come from within. We urged them to focus on developing their inner strength, resilience, and compassion. By cultivating a positive mindset and embracing their own uniqueness, they could build a bright and fulfilling future.

We also stressed the importance of self-acceptance and self-love. By loving and accepting themselves as they are, they would be better equipped to face life's challenges with confidence and grace. We encouraged them to set goals, pursue their passions, and surround themselves with supportive and loving people.

.

Through our efforts to mentor and support these teens, we found a renewed sense of purpose. We realized that by lifting others up, we also lifted ourselves, creating a ripple effect of positivity and transformation in our communities. The impact of our words and actions was evident in the newfound confidence and hope we saw in the eyes of those we helped.

Our journey had come full circle. From a young person struggling with self-doubt and insecurity to an empowered individual offering guidance and support, we had discovered the true meaning of resilience and inner beauty. And in helping others see their own worth, we continued to heal and grow, knowing that our experiences had not been in vain.

Chapter 11: Celebrating Milestones and Achievements

Along the way, we celebrated countless milestones and achievements, both big and small. From personal triumphs to professional successes, each accomplishment served as a reminder of how far we had come and how much we were capable of achieving. We savored these moments of joy and gratitude, knowing that they were a testament to our resilience, determination, and unwavering belief in ourselves.

One of the most significant milestones came when we finally welcomed not just one, but two beautiful boys into our family. After the heartbreak of miscarriage, the arrival of our sons felt like a divine blessing—a reaffirmation of hope and the promise of new beginnings. They were born three years apart, each a unique and cherished addition to our family.

With their arrival, it felt as though God had shown Himself upon our lives once again. The feelings of uncertainty and inadequacy that had plagued us for so long were replaced with wonder and joy. We marveled at the miracle of life and the precious gift of motherhood, grateful for the opportunity to nurture and love these precious souls.

As we watched our boys grow and thrive, everything seemed to fall into place. Our family felt complete, filled with love, laughter, and endless possibilities. The challenges we had faced along the way had only served to strengthen our bond and deepen our appreciation for the blessings we had been given.

The journey to parenthood had been marked by trials and tribulations, but it had also been filled with moments of profound joy and fulfillment. Our sons brought light and happiness into our lives, reminding us of the beauty of new beginnings and the power of love to overcome any obstacle.

As we celebrated this milestone, we were filled with gratitude for the journey that had led us to this moment. We had overcome adversity, embraced change, and emerged stronger and more resilient than ever before. And as we looked to the future, we did so with hope and optimism, knowing that whatever challenges lay ahead, we would face them together, as a family.

Chapter 12 Embracing the Future

Today, I can tell you that the journey was worth it. Though we faced many challenges, we emerged stronger and wiser. Our dreams may have evolved, but they are still very much alive. And now, we approach life with a balanced confidence, grounded in self-acceptance and resilience.

As I reflect on the journey that brought me to this point, I can't help but feel a sense of sorrow for the ways in which I let down my younger self along the way. I'm sorry for not standing up for her, for not pursuing her dreams with the determination and courage she deserved. I'm sorry for allowing the world to intimidate her, for letting fear hold her back from embracing her true potential.

There were moments when I faltered, when I allowed self-doubt and insecurity to cloud my judgment and hinder my progress. But through it all, I never lost sight of the strength and resilience that had carried me through the darkest times. And though I may have stumbled along the way, I never stopped striving to become the person I knew I was capable of being.

To my younger self, I offer my sincerest apologies for not always being the advocate and champion you needed. But I also offer my deepest gratitude for your unwavering resilience and determination. You may have faced setbacks and challenges, but you never lost sight of your dreams. And because of that, I stand here today, stronger and more empowered than ever before.

As I look to the future, I do so with a renewed sense of purpose and determination. I am committed to honoring the dreams and aspirations of my younger self, to pursuing them with unwavering courage and conviction. I will not allow fear or self-doubt to hold me back any longer. Instead, I will embrace each new opportunity with open arms, knowing that with perseverance and faith, anything is possible.

So, to my younger self, I say this: I am sorry for the times I let you down, but I promise to make it right. I will carry your dreams forward with me, always striving to live a life that would make you proud. And together, we will continue to embrace the future with hope, courage, and unwavering belief in the power of our dreams.

Conclusion:

As we reach the end of this journey together, I am reminded of the words of poet Rumi: "The wound is the place where the light enters you." Throughout the pages of this book, we have explored the depths of pain and struggle, but we have also witnessed the transformative power of resilience, hope, and love.

My story is not just my own—it is a testament to the universal human experience, a reminder that we all face challenges and setbacks on our journey through life. But it is also a testament to the incredible strength and resilience that lies within each of us, waiting to be awakened in the face of adversity.

Through the ups and downs, the triumphs and tribulations, I have learned that the most important journey we can undertake is the journey to self-discovery and self-acceptance. It is a journey marked by moments of courage, vulnerability, and growth—a journey that ultimately leads us back to ourselves, to the core of our being where true happiness and fulfillment reside.

As we close the chapter on this book, I am filled with gratitude for the opportunity to share my story with you. I hope that my words have served as a source of inspiration and encouragement, reminding you that no matter what challenges you may face, you are never alone.

May you carry the lessons learned from these pages with you on your own journey, embracing each new experience with an open heart and a resilient spirit. And may you always remember that within you lies the power to overcome any obstacle and to create a life filled with purpose, joy, and fulfillment.

Thank you for joining me on this journey. May your path be illuminated by the light of hope, guided by the wisdom of resilience, and enriched by the beauty of self-discovery.

With heartfelt gratitude and best wishes for the road ahead,

Eva Itumeleng Malinga

Book Description

"Letters to My Younger Self: A Journey of Resilience and Rediscovery" is a heartfelt and inspiring narrative that delves into the transformative journey of a young woman who once brimmed with confidence and dreams, only to face the harsh realities of life that threatened to dim her inner light. This compelling memoir, written in the form of letters to her younger self, offers a deeply personal and candid reflection on the struggles and triumphs that have shaped her life.

From the innocent optimism of childhood to the turbulent years of adolescence marked by self-doubt and the painful loss of her mother, the author shares her experiences with raw honesty and vulnerability. Each chapter unveils the challenges she faced—academic struggles, the onset of acne, and a crippling lack of confidence that led to missed opportunities and a profound sense of loss.

Yet, amid the darkness, there are moments of hope and redemption. The author recounts meeting the love of her life, whose unwavering support helped her rediscover her self-worth and reignite her dreams. She speaks of the joy and fulfillment found in motherhood, despite the heartbreak of miscarriages, and the strength she gained through her faith and acceptance of Jesus as her savior.

As she navigates the complexities of adulthood, the author learns to embrace her uniqueness, finding beauty and strength in her reflection. She offers heartfelt advice to teens grappling with similar struggles, urging them to look beyond appearances and focus on their inner strength and potential.

In a powerful conclusion, the author reflects on the importance of resilience and self-love, expressing regret for not standing up for her younger self sooner but also recognizing the journey's profound impact on her growth. She dedicates this book to her teenage daughter, Bonolo, and to all teens struggling with confidence, hoping her story will inspire and empower them to overcome their challenges and embrace their true selves.

"Letters to My Younger Self" is not just a memoir; it is a testament to the human spirit's resilience and the transformative power of love, faith, and self-acceptance. It is a beacon of hope for anyone who has ever felt lost, reminding us that our greatest struggles can lead to our most significant triumphs.